help and

sey.com

most
ritish
isles. .... miles (160 kms) south of mainland Britain yet only 14 miles (22 kms) from the coast of France, Jersey provides a remarkable variety of environment and attractions. Despite its small size – Jersey measures just nine miles by five (14 kms x 8 kms) - all your senses are made to work overtime in this tiny Island

JERSEY

A Little Souvenir

CHRIS ANDREWS PUBLICATIONS

Corbiére Lighthouse

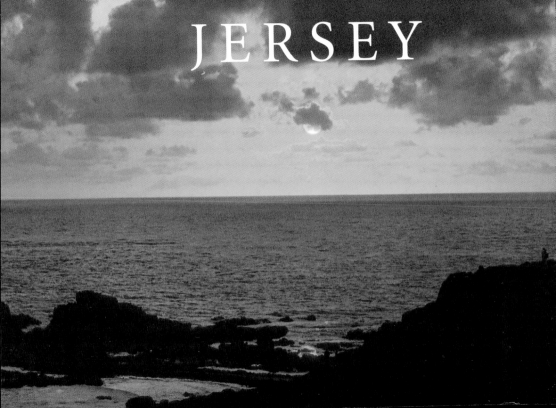

JERSEY

Introduction

Jersey is the British Isles' most southerly outpost, it lies just 14 miles (22kms) west of Normandy's Cotentin Peninsula and at 45 square miles (72km), is the largest Channel Island.

Her loyalty may lie to the north, but the island looks longingly southward. A southerly aspect and mild climate makes this one of Britain's balmiest corners.

Victor Hugo's declaration that the Channel Islands are *"Fragments of France which fell into the sea and were gathered up by England"* is particularly poignant here. Early records tell of two French saints visiting Jersey without crossing anything more than a "simple brook". Separation finally occurred around 709AD.

But Jersey has been shaped by more than the elements. Her character is a rare distillation of two distinct cultures, blended with an independent island spirit. Jersey's British pedigree dates from 1066, when the Norman Channel Islands helped Duke

Cottages at St Brelade's Bay 5

William to conquer England. When King John lost his Norman lands in 1204, islanders remained loyal to the Crown in exchange for rights and privileges that remain unchanged to this day. French was the island's official language until the 1960s and *Jersiais*, Jersey's Norman patois, can still be heard.

The self-governing Bailiwick of Jersey is divided into 12 parishes, each with its own character. Nature lovers are spoiled, with everything from St

Ouen's acclaimed sand dunes to the lush, green valley of St Peter on offer, along with cliffs and hedgerows teeming with wildlife, plus sleepy, rural views that seem far too big for the island.

Walkers relish the dramatic, plunging beauty of Jersey's northern cliffs, whilst the east coast offers a Moon Walk: 12m tides add an extra 40 percent to the island's area, affording guided treks across the ocean floor. Leafy lanes and bracing, west coast paths complete this pedestrian paradise.

There's a Jersey beach to suit everyone. St Ouen's Bay, a British surfing Mecca, offers a striking contrast to sheltered coves like Portelet. St Brelade's Bay exudes Mediterranean chic whilst bucket-and-spade favourites like Grève de Lecq and Royal Bay of Grouville are perfect for family beach holidays.

St Ouen's Bay

Jersey's two offshore reefs, Les Minquiers and Les Ecrehous, are havens of tranquillity, where white-washed cottages cling to tiny outcrops. Together they support seals, dolphins and desert-like stretches of low-tide sand.

Jersey is where past and present meet. The parish of St Lawrence is home to Hamptonne Country Life Museum, Le Rât Cottage and the Jersey War Tunnels, which, together, form a living link to a bygone island. La Hougue Bie, St Saviour's Neolithic

burial mound topped by two medieval chapels, provides a brooding backdrop to a moving WWII memorial bunker, whilst Elizabeth Castle, built to repel French invaders and accessible by amphibious truck, is an historic counterpoint to St Helier's modern waterfront development.

Jersey Zoo, in the Parish of Trinity, is globally acclaimed for its pioneering conservation and breeding of endangered species, whilst St Helier's cosmopolitan shopping, cafès, covered market and museums draw locals and visitors alike. Add around 200 places to eat out, a wealth of attractions including a working vineyard plus, of course, the world famous Jersey Cow and the result is an enchanting and unforgettable island experience.

Flowers at the Tourism Centre in St Helier 11

12   Elizabeth Castle and St Helier from the sea

Liberation Monument and the marina in St Helier   13

14　New development at St Helier Harbour

16   St Aubin's Bay

St Aubin   17

18   St Aubin's Harbour

20   St Brelade's Bay

22 St Brelade's Bay with a cottage and the Chuch with its 11th Century Fisherman's Chapel

Fisherman off Fiquet Bay   23

Clear Jersey sea

26　St Ouen's Bay, a huge sandy beach to the west, beloved of surfers and holidaymakers

Memorial to a successful rescue and a beach flag at St Ouen   27

28   The well known surf at St Ouen

Lecq Farm, a typical Jersey longhouse 29

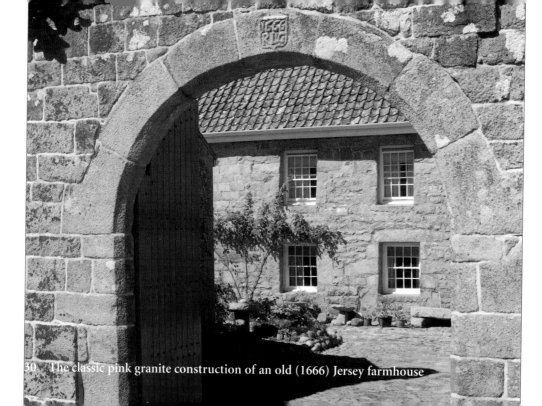

30 The classic pink granite construction of an old (1666) Jersey farmhouse

32　Grève de Lecq, the popular north coast beach

Fishermen's tractors and boats at Grève de Lecq   33

34   Grève de Lecq

The coast in early summer   35

36   Jersey Cows in St John

38   The north coast looking west

The north coast looking east

Plemont to Grosnez Point

42   Jersey flowers and farmhouse

Floral display on The Royal in St Martin's   43

44 Sweet Corn in fields above the coast

One of the many pleasant paths for walkers to enjoy

46 Rose hips and Bouley Bay

Wave flow over the steps at Bouley Bay   47

48   Jersey phone box

Heron on a quite corner of the Handois Reservoir   49

50   Flamingos at Durrel Wildlife Conservation Trust

Gorilla and marmoset at Durrel   51

52   Jersey orchids

The vines at La Mare Vineyard and the urn containing a bottle from the first vintage   53

54 St Catherine's over Anne Port

56   St Catherine's breakwater

58   The gardens at Samarès Manor

60   Mount Orgueil Castle and Gorey

Medieval display and visitors in the castle   61

62 Gorey Harbour

Artist on the wall at Gorey 63

First published 2007 by Chris Andrews Publications
15 Curtis Yard North Hinksey Lane Oxford OX2 0LX
Telephone: +44(0)1865 723404 **www.cap-ox.com**
Photos: Chris Andrews with Sue Daly Text: Marco Ciotti © Chris Andrews Publications
ISBN 978–1-905385-39-3

Front Cover: St Brelade's Bay Title page: Jersey Cow This page: Corbière Lighthouse Back cover: St Aubin's Bay